Prolance

www.prolancewriting.com
California, USA
©2017 Prolance
ISBN: 978-0-9987527-2-3

Believe

The Dos & Don'ts of the Quran

Forward

Allah gave us the Quran.

5:15-16 *There has come to you from God a light and a luminous Book, through which God, by His grace, guides all who seek His good pleasure on the path of peace, and brings them out of the depths of darkness into light and guides them unto a Straight Path.*

6:114 *Then is it other than Allah I should seek as judge while it is He who has revealed to you the Book explained in detail? And those to whom We [previously] gave the Scripture know that it is sent down from your Lord in truth, so never be among the doubters.*

Allah sent down His message through the beloved Prophet Mohamed (peace be upon him).

33:41 *Mohamed is not the father of any of your men, but he is the Messenger of Allah and the seal of the Prophets and Allah has full knowledge of all things.*

46:9 *Say (O Mohamed), "I am not a novelty among other messengers, nor do I know what will happen to me or to you. I follow nothing other than what is revealed to me (Quran). I am no more than a clear warner.*

I like lists.

A lot.

It's how my brain organizes information. As I maneuvered my way through the English translation of the Quran throughout this year I started to write down all the dos and dont's in order to allow my brain to filter through all the religious information I've learned from my teenage years into adulthood.

Since the Quran is truly complete, clear, and includes all things, then why not have a concise list? I thought.

What does the Quran ask of me?
What are God's guidelines?

So I read, very slowly. A year to read a 433-page book, verse by verse - a lot of times repeatedly - many times, confirming and reconfirming with other translations.

My intention while accumulating was for personal use. It was my list. Of the other 25 lists in my life that help me maneuver through my work tasks, household duties, etc, this one would be the most important.

And when I was done, I simply wanted to pay it forward.

Contents

*May God forgive any
shortcomings in this book.*

worship

1. Believe in God; faith.   (2:3... ...)
2. Believe in the Quran.   (2:4...)
3. Have absolute faith in the afterlife. (2:4... ...)
4. Do not worship other gods but   (...31:13...)
   God; idolatry.
5. Believe in the angels.   (2:177...)
6. Believe in the prophets.   (2:177...)
7. Believe that Jesus was a prophet,   (4:171)
   not God and not God's son.
8. Submit to God.   (3:20...)
9. Do not worship angels.   (37:80)
10. Do not worship prophets.   (37:80)
11. Avoid divination.   (5:90)
12. Repent.   (...25:71...)
13. Do not fear man in terms of   (5:44...)
    judgments, only fear God.
14. Do not hold this life in higher   (...13:38...)
    esteem than the next.
15. Always remember that God has   (...49:16...)
    knowledge of all your actions and
    thoughts.
16. Do not let Satan deceive you.   (2:208...)
17. Obey God, the apostle and   (...4:59...)
    those in authority.

18. Fast in Ramadan, unless you are sick or traveling. (2:185)

19. Perform Hajj/pilgrimage to Mecca. (22:27)

20. Do not hunt animals while on pilgrimage. (5:96)

21. Pray the daily prayers. (...24:58...)

22. Do not approach prayer while drunk. (4:43)

23. Attend to your prayers promptly. (2:238)

24. When you rise to pray wash: face, hands to elbows, wipe your head and wash feet till ankles. (5:6)

25. If no water is available for cleaning, use sand to rub hands and face. (5:6)

26. If you are in a state of impurity, wash the whole body (bathe). (5:6)

27. Pray neither secretly nor in private, find a middle course. (17:110)

28. You can shorten your prayers during travel. (4:101)

29. You can shorten your prayer if under attack. (4:101)

30. Turn to the correct direction for prayer. (2:144)

31. Be steadfast in belief to God, (2:154)
even when evil befalls you.
32. When summoned to Friday (6:29)
prayer, cease your trading and
hasten to the remembrance of
God.
33. Be thankful to God. (...2:252...)
34. Do not talk of future events (18:24)
without saying, "If God wills."
35. Proclaim God's greatness. (...56:96...)
36. Do not say falsehoods about (16:116)
God.
37. When the Quran is read, listen (7:204)
to it with attention
38. If you hear falsehoods about (4:140)
God, or the Quran, do not
stay silent.
39. Do not forbid the things that (5:87)
God has made lawful.
40. Invoke blessings on the Prophet (33:57)
Mohamed (pbuh).

41. When called to war, men must (4:95)
go except the blind, mentally
deficient or sick.
42. Follow the rules of war outlined. (...4:75...)

character

1. Be patient. (2:153...)
2. Be true to your promises. (...17:34...)
3. Do not break an oath. (5:89...)
4. Do not knowingly lie or conceal truth. (2:42...)
5. Do not initiate aggression. (2:190)
6. Do not steal. (4:29...)
7. Be righteous. (2:177)
8. Be trustworthy. (4:58)
9. Forgive. (3:134)
10. Curb your anger. (3:134)
11. Be kind: To parents, family, orphans, destitute, neighbors, travelers in need, slaves and friends. (4:36...)
12. Do not be arrogant. (7:146)
13. Do not be boastful. (4:36)
14. Be humble. (25:63...)
15. Judge people with fairness. (4:135)
16. Do not use harsh words; Profanity (...4:148...)
17. Do not be proud. (..16:23...)
18. Do not be scornful. (31:18...)
19. Be just. (...5:8...)
20. Do not be immoral or lewd in a sexual manner. (6:151)

21.	Be courteous in speech.	(4:86...)
22.	Do not gossip or pay heed to gossip or idle talk.	(...17:36...)
23.	Do not slander.	(24:16)
24.	Do not be wasteful.	(17:27)
25.	Do not be miserly; stingy.	(70:21)
26.	Do not be prodigal; extravagant.	(7:31)
27.	Endure adversity with fortitude.	(42:44)
28.	Be chaste.	(33:35...)
29.	Be generous.	(2:272...)
30.	Do not engage in vain disputes.	(74:45)
31.	Do not backbite.	(49:12)
32.	Do not spy.	(49:12)
33.	Do not mock.	(49:11)
34.	Do not defame.	(49:11)
35.	Avoid being overly suspicious.	(49:12)
36.	Be clean.	(2:222)
37.	Bestow no favors expecting gain.	(74:6)
38.	Let your stride be modest.	(31:19)
39.	Let your voice be low.	(31:19)
40.	Do not spread corruption.	(2:11...)
41.	Do not prevent people from worshiping or entering Mosques.	(2:114)
42.	Cover the faults of others.	(2:263)

giving
& taking

1. Leave your earnings and property properly and justly according to the rules outlined. (4:7...)
2. Do not give in charity to impress other people. (107:6)
3. Give from your wealth to your family, orphans, poor, travelers, captives and beggars. (2:177... ...)
4. Give from what you love. (3:92)
5. Do not hoard. (47:38)
6. Give charity in public and private, but privately is better. (2:271...)
7. Pay your alms levy. (2:3... ... ...)
8. Pay alms to: Poor, destitute, managers of alms, those who are faithful, towards freeing a slave, debt, to advance God's cause or to a traveler in need. (9:60)
9. Do not partake in usury. (4:161)
10. Write down debts in a contract. (2:282)

relationships

1. Do not wed a pagan. (2:221)
2. Follow the rules of divorce (...2:226...) outlined.
3. Widows must wait 4 months and (2:234) 10 days before remarrying.
4. A man can marry a Christian or (5:5) Jewish woman.
5. If you marry more than one wife, (4:3) be just among them.
6. Give wives a dowry. (4:4)
7. Do not take back a dowry upon (4:20) divorce.
8. Husbands be kind to your wives. (4:19)
9. Do not wed women against their (4:19) will.
10. Do not marry a woman your (4:22) father has married.
11. During a disagreement between (4:35) spouses, bring one relative from each side to arbitrate.
12. Guard your private parts from (23:5) unlawful sexual temptations.
13. Do not commit adultery. (17:32)
14. Do not have intercourse with (2:187) your spouses while fasting.

15. Do not have intercourse during the menstruation time of a woman. (2:222)

16. Do not vow to abstain sexually from your spouses for more than 4 months. (2:226)

17. Men should not lust after men, or fornicate with them. (7:81)

18. Restrain your sexual desires except with spouses. (23:6)

19. Do not take on mistresses. (5:5)

20. Do not wed those with blood relations as outlined. (4:23)

21. Husband must maintain his family financially according to his means. (4:34)

22. Do not spread sexual rumors about women. (24:4)

23. Do not enter people's homes without permission and salute them with peace in the name of God upon entering. (24:27)

24. When greeted return the greeting or make it better. (4:86)

Friends

25. Surround yourself with like-minded, positive people; believers. (4:69)
26. Be courteous with non-Muslims. (60:8)
27. A mother is encouraged to breastfeed for 2 years. (2:223)

Children

28. Do not kill unwanted children in fear of poverty. (17:31)
29. Name your adopted sons or daughters after their biological fathers. (33:5)
30. Deal with orphans justly. (4:2...)

Parents

31. Let not your riches or children divert you from God. (63:9)
32. Honor your parents. (...29:8...)
33. Treat aging parents with patience, kind words, humility and tenderness. (17:23)
34. Pray for your parents to have mercy from God. (17:24)
35. Do not obey your parents if they ask you to serve another god. (31:15)

Death

36. Do not kill. (6:151...)
37. Do not kill yourself. (4:29)
38. Bury the dead. (5:31)

eating
& dressing

1. Do not eat decaying flesh, blood or swine. (5:3)

2. Do not drink alcohol. (2:219...)

3. Do not eat flesh slaughtered and dedicated to another god or idols.

4. Do not eat the flesh of strangled, gorged or beaten animals. (5:3)

5. If you are constrained to hunger, it's ok to eat what is forbidden. (5:3)

6. Do not eat or drink in excess. (7:31)

7. Dress modestly. (...7:26)

8. Women, draw your veils (kerchiefs) over your chest (bosoms). (24:31) (24:31)

9. Women, do not display your attractiveness (adornments) except to husbands, fathers, brothers...as outlined. (24:31)

10. Women, do not stomp your feet to reveal hidden body parts. (24:31)

إِلَّا مَنْ تَابَ وَآمَنَ وَعَمِلَ عَمَلًا صَالِحًا فَأُولَٰئِكَ يُبَدِّلُ اللَّهُ سَيِّئَاتِهِمْ حَسَنَاتٍ ۗ وَكَانَ اللَّهُ غَفُورًا رَحِيمًا

Save him who repents and believes and does good works; as for such, Allah will change their evil deeds to good deeds. Allah is ever Forgiving, Merciful.

Chapter 25, Verse 70

References:
The Koran; N.J. Dawood; Penguin Classics
The Study Quran; Seyyed Hossein Nasr; HarperOne
www.quran.com

www.ingramcontent.com/pod-product-compliance
Lightning Source LLC
Chambersburg PA
CBHW060747100426
42813CB00004B/728